contents

NZ, Canada, US and UK readers
Please note that Australian cup and spoon
measurements are metric. A quick conversion
guide appears on page 63.

about the wok

While you don't need a wok to stir-fry successfully, it certainly is an advantage. The large round open shape is designed especially to conduct the high heat needed for rapid cooking, and to help move food around with ease. Here's what you need to know about the wok and its accessories.

Which wok to buy?

Woks come in a variety of shapes, sizes and finishes, ranging from the traditional carbon steel wok to cast-iron, stainless steel, non-stick and electric ones. The traditional round-based wok is great for gas burners, while the flat-based wok is best used on electric stoves. You can buy woks from Asian food stores and department stores.

Seasoning a wok

Stainless steel and non-stick woks don't need seasoning. However, carbon steel and cast-iron woks need to be seasoned before use. First, wash the wok in hot soapy water to remove all traces of grease, then dry it thoroughly. Heat the wok, add about 2 tablespoons of cooking oil and rub over the entire inside surface of the wok with absorbent paper.

Continue heating the wok for about 10 to 15 minutes, wiping with more paper; cool. Repeat this process twice. The wok is now ready to use. After each use, wash the wok in hot, soapy water; do not scrub it with steel wool or harsh abrasives. Dry the wok thoroughly by standing it over low heat for a few minutes, then rub or spray a thin layer of cooking oil over the entire surface before storing, to prevent rust.

With constant use, the inside surface will darken and become well-seasoned. The older, more seasoned the wok becomes, the easier it will be to use.

Wok chan
A wok spatula (or chan) is a metal, shovel-like utensil used for lifting, tossing and stirring food. Its great disadvantage is the noise it makes. A wooden spatula is better for non-stick woks as it won't scratch the surface.

Wok burners
Many cooktops incorporate wok burners or you can have one specially fitted into your benchtop. You can buy portable gas wok burners and wok accessory kits for barbecues. A wok holder or ring is a metal band which you place over an electric element to hold the wok in place.

from left: flat-based wok for electric stove, sitting on wok holder; traditional wok with lid, chan and cleaver.

Stir-frying tips

- Prepare all ingredients before you start to cook.
- For best results, cut meat across the grain as thinly as possible. To do this, wrap meat tightly in plastic wrap then partly freeze before cutting it into wafer-thin slices.
- Heat the wok before adding oil, then add the food immediately.
- Stir-fry meat, poultry and seafood over high heat, in batches, so the food will brown and seal quickly, rather than stew.
- It is important to keep lifting, stirring and moving ingredients in the wok while stir-frying. A wok chan or a wooden spatula is ideal for this. You should also shake the wok while stir-frying. To do this, hold the handle in one hand (wear an oven glove for protection against the heat). You will soon coordinate the shaking and stir-fry actions.
- Stir-fry just before serving.

4 beef and snake beans

with vermicelli

250g rice vermicelli noodles

2 teaspoons sesame oil

2 medium (300g) onions,
sliced

2 tablespoons red
wine vinegar

1 tablespoon brown sugar

1 tablespoon peanut oil

600g beef strips

2 teaspoons grated
fresh ginger

3 cloves garlic, crushed

1/4 cup (60ml) hoisin sauce

2 tablespoons salt-reduced
soy sauce

2 tablespoons chopped fresh
coriander leaves

250g snake beans, chopped

1 tablespoon sesame seeds

Place noodles in heatproof bowl, cover
with boiling water; stand 5 minutes, drain.
Heat half the sesame oil in wok or
large pan; stir-fry onions, vinegar and
sugar, over low heat, until onions are
caramelised, remove from pan.
Heat peanut oil in same pan; stir-fry beef,
in batches, until browned and tender.
Heat remaining sesame oil in same pan;
stir-fry ginger, garlic, sauces, coriander,
beans and seeds until beans are just
tender. Return beef and onions to pan
with noodles; stir-fry until heated through.

6 broad beans, chickpeas and lemon thyme with noodles

1/3 cup (80ml) olive oil

1 large (200g) onion, chopped

3 medium (600g) red capsicums, chopped

2 cloves garlic, crushed

3 medium (570g) tomatoes, peeled, seeded, chopped

1 cup (250ml) vegetable stock

1 teaspoon sugar

300g can chickpeas, rinsed, drained

500g frozen broad beans, cooked, peeled

1 1/2 tablespoons chopped fresh lemon thyme

1/3 cup (25g) finely grated parmesan cheese

250g thick dried egg noodles

1/2 cup (40g) parmesan cheese flakes

Heat oil in wok or large pan; stir-fry onion, capsicum and garlic until onion is soft. Add tomatoes; stir-fry 10 minutes. Add stock, sugar and chickpeas; cook, covered, 5 minutes. Add broad beans, thyme and grated cheese; stir-fry until heated through.

Meanwhile, cook noodles in large pan of boiling water, uncovered, until just tender; drain.

Add noodles to vegetable mixture in pan, toss gently; top with cheese.

teriyaki chicken

with green beans

1 tablespoon
peanut oil

3 (500g) chicken
breast fillets, sliced

200g green beans,
halved

1/2 cup (125ml) water

2 tablespoons black
bean sauce

1 tablespoon sweet
chilli sauce

1 tablespoon
teriyaki sauce

1 clove garlic, crushed

2 teaspoons grated
fresh ginger

1 medium (150g)
onion, sliced thinly

400g bok choy, sliced

1 1/4 cups (100g)
bean sprouts

Heat oil in wok or
large pan; stir-fry
chicken, in batches,
until browned. Return
chicken to pan with
beans, water, sauces,
garlic, ginger and
onion; stir-fry until
beans are tender.
Add bok choy and
bean sprouts; stir-fry
until heated through.

8 creamy chicken stir-fry

Boil, steam or microwave broccoli until just tender; drain. Heat oil in wok or large pan; stir-fry chicken, in batches, until browned lightly. Return chicken to pan with onion and capsicum; stir-fry 2 minutes or until onion is soft.

Pour 2 tablespoons coconut milk into a small bowl; add remaining milk with sauce, sambal oelek, sugar, coriander and broccoli to pan. Stir-fry until mixture is heated through.

Blend cornflour with reserved coconut milk, add to pan, stir over heat until mixture boils and thickens; stir in bean sprouts.

400g broccoli, chopped

1 tablespoon peanut oil

5 (550g) chicken thigh fillets, sliced

1 medium (150g) onion, chopped

1 medium (200g) red capsicum, sliced

400ml can coconut milk

1 tablespoon fish sauce

1 teaspoon sambal oelek

1½ tablespoons caster sugar

1 tablespoon chopped fresh coriander leaves

1 tablespoon cornflour

¾ cup (60g) bean sprouts

Microwave Broccoli suitable

tofu and vegetable stir-fry

350g cauliflower, chopped

350g broccoli, chopped

250g asparagus, sliced

350g green beans, sliced

3 medium (360g) carrots, sliced

1/4 cup (60ml) olive oil

2 cloves garlic, crushed

1 tablespoon chopped fresh thyme

1 teaspoon cracked black pepper

375g firm tofu, cubed

2 medium (300g) onions, sliced

250g button mushrooms, sliced

1 vegetable stock cube

1 tablespoon cornflour

1/2 cup dry white wine

1 cup (250ml) water

1/4 cup (20g) grated parmesan cheese

Add cauliflower, broccoli, asparagus, beans and carrots to large pan of boiling water; boil, uncovered, 2 minutes, drain. Rinse under cold water; drain.

Heat oil in wok or large pan; stir-fry garlic, thyme, pepper and tofu until tofu is browned lightly, remove from pan.

Add onions and mushrooms to same pan; stir-fry until onions are soft. Stir in vegetable mixture, wine, crumbled stock cube and blended cornflour and water; stir over heat until mixture boils and thickens. Stir in tofu; serve sprinkled with cheese.

chicken and egg noodle
stir-fry

350g thin fresh
egg noodles

1 tablespoon peanut oil

6 (660g) chicken thigh
fillets, sliced

1 teaspoon finely grated
fresh ginger

1 small fresh red chilli,
sliced thinly

1 small (80g) onion, sliced

1 medium (120g)
carrot, sliced

3 (100g) Chinese
sausages, sliced

1 teaspoon peanut
oil, extra

4 eggs, beaten lightly

2 teaspoons salt-reduced
soy sauce

1 tablespoon
oyster sauce

1/4 cup (60ml)
chicken stock

1/4 teaspoon sesame oil

crunchy shrimp topping

4 green onions, sliced

1 clove garlic, crushed

1/4 cup dried
shrimp, chopped

Rinse noodles under cold water; drain. Heat half the peanut oil in wok or large pan; stir-fry chicken, in batches, until browned and tender. Heat remaining peanut oil in same pan; stir-fry ginger, chilli, onion, carrot and sausages until carrot is tender; remove from pan.

Heat half the extra peanut oil in wok or large pan; add half the eggs, swirl pan so eggs form a thin omelette. Cook until set, remove from pan; cool. Repeat with remaining extra peanut oil and eggs. Roll omelettes firmly, cut into thin slices.

Return chicken to pan with vegetable mixture, omelette slices, noodles and remaining ingredients; stir-fry until heated through. Serve sprinkled with Crunchy Shrimp Topping.

Crunchy Shrimp Topping Add onions, garlic and shrimp to wok or pan; stir-fry until heated through.

12 beef with
oyster sauce

400g bok choy

*1/2 bunch
Chinese broccoli*

*2 tablespoons
peanut oil*

*2 cloves garlic,
crushed*

500g beef strips

150g snow peas

*425g can baby corn,
drained*

*6 green onions,
chopped*

*2 tablespoons
oyster sauce*

*1 tablespoon
fish sauce*

1 tablespoon sugar

Cut bok choy and broccoli into large pieces; boil, steam or microwave, separately, until just tender; drain. Cover to keep warm.
Heat oil in wok or large pan; stir-fry garlic and beef until browned. Add snow peas, corn, onions, sauces and sugar to same pan; stir-fry until snow peas are just tender. Serve over bok choy and broccoli.

Microwave Bok choy and broccoli suitable

mustard pork with

olives and artichokes

2 tablespoons olive oil

500g pork fillets, sliced

2 tablespoons red wine vinegar

2 tablespoons Dijon mustard

1 tablespoon soy sauce

1 clove garlic, crushed

2 teaspoons sugar

2 medium (340g) red onions, sliced

500g spinach, chopped roughly

400g can artichoke hearts, drained, halved

1/2 cup sun-dried tomatoes in oil, drained, halved

1/2 cup (60g) pitted black olives

Heat half the oil in wok or large pan; stir-fry combined pork, vinegar, mustard, sauce, garlic and sugar, in batches, until pork is browned. **Heat** remaining oil in same pan; stir-fry onions until just soft. Return pork to pan with spinach, artichokes, tomatoes and olives; stir-fry until spinach is wilted.

14 spicy honeyed squid

4 (880g) squid hoods

2 tablespoons
vegetable oil

2 cloves garlic,
crushed

1½ tablespoons
honey

1½ tablespoons
maple-flavoured syrup

1½ tablespoons
white vinegar

1½ tablespoons
chopped fresh parsley

1½ tablespoons
chopped fresh
basil leaves

2 teaspoons chopped
fresh thyme

2 teaspoons
Tabasco sauce

½ teaspoon
celery salt

Cut squid hoods open, cut shallow diagonal
slashes in criss-cross pattern on inside surface;
cut into 2cm x 8cm pieces.
Heat half the oil in wok or large pan; stir-fry
garlic and half the squid for 1 minute, remove
from pan. Repeat with remaining oil and squid.
Return squid to pan with remaining ingredients;
stir-fry for 3 minutes or until squid is tender.

black bean,

beef and asparagus

750g beef strips

1 tablespoon rice vinegar

1 tablespoon soy sauce

1 tablespoon dry sherry

2 cloves garlic, crushed

2 tablespoons peanut oil

1½ tablespoons salted dried black beans

2 medium (300g) onions, sliced thickly

500g asparagus, halved

1 teaspoon cornflour

2 tablespoons oyster sauce

⅓ cup (80ml) beef stock

Combine beef, vinegar, sauce, sherry and garlic in medium bowl. Cover; refrigerate 10 minutes. Heat half the oil in wok or large pan; stir-fry beef, in batches, until browned and almost cooked.

Rinse beans, drain, mash with fork. Heat remaining oil in same pan; stir-fry beans, onions and asparagus until onions are almost soft. Return beef to pan, stir in blended cornflour, oyster sauce and stock; stir over heat until mixture boils and thickens slightly.

stir-fried udon

and crispy lamb

1 clove garlic, crushed

1/2 cup (125ml) hoisin sauce

1 tablespoon soy sauce

1 tablespoon sweet chilli sauce

1 tablespoon oyster sauce

750g whole piece lamb eye of loin, cut into thin strips

plain flour

vegetable oil, for deep-frying

350g udon noodles

2 tablespoons water

500g choy sum

Combine garlic and sauces in large bowl to make a marinade;
reserve 2 tablespoons of marinade. Add lamb to bowl; coat with
remaining marinade. Cover; refrigerate 10 minutes.

Drain lamb; discard marinade. Toss lamb in flour; shake off excess.
Heat oil in wok or large pan; deep-fry lamb, in batches, until browned
and crisp. Drain on absorbent paper; cover to keep warm.

Cook noodles in large pan of boiling water, uncovered, until just tender;
drain. Rinse under cold water; drain.

Combine reserved marinade and water in clean wok or large pan;
add choy sum and stir-fry until just wilted. Remove choy sum mixture;
cover to keep warm. Add noodles to same pan; stir-fry until heated
through. Divide noodles among serving plates; top with choy sum
then crispy lamb.

18 marinated beef
with spicy barbecue sauce

800g beef strips

2 cloves garlic, crushed

3 small fresh red chillies, chopped

500g asparagus, chopped

250g fresh baby corn, halved

2 tablespoons peanut oil

1 large (350g) red capsicum, sliced thinly

2 tablespoons plum sauce

1/4 cup (60ml) Chinese barbecue sauce

2 teaspoons rice vinegar

2 tablespoons tomato paste

Combine beef, garlic and chillies in bowl; mix well. Boil, steam or microwave asparagus and corn, separately, until just tender; rinse under cold water, drain.

Heat oil in wok or large pan; stir-fry beef mixture, in batches, until beef is browned and tender. Return beef to pan with asparagus, corn, capsicum and combined sauces, vinegar and tomato paste; stir-fry until mixture boils.

Microwave Asparagus and corn suitable

stir-fried mushrooms, beans and bok choy

1 teaspoon sesame oil

1 tablespoon vegetable oil

400g bok choy, shredded coarsely

½ medium (300g) Chinese cabbage, shredded coarsely

450g broccoli, chopped

100g shiitake mushrooms, halved

150g oyster mushrooms, halved

300g can red kidney beans, rinsed, drained

⅓ cup (80ml) hoisin sauce

¼ cup (60ml) lime juice

¼ cup (60ml) orange juice

Heat oils in wok or large pan; stir-fry bok choy and cabbage until just wilted. Add broccoli, mushrooms, beans, sauce and juices to same pan; cook, covered, about 3 minutes or until broccoli is just tender.

20 spicy prawns

1kg medium uncooked prawns

1 tablespoon peanut oil

Marinade

2 cloves garlic, crushed

2 teaspoons grated fresh ginger

2 teaspoons finely chopped fresh lemon grass

$1/2$ teaspoon ground cumin

$1/2$ teaspoon ground coriander

1 tablespoon teriyaki sauce

2 teaspoons honey

4 green onions, chopped

$1/2$ teaspoon sambal oelek

Shell and devein prawns, leaving tails intact. Combine prawns and Marinade in large bowl; mix well. Cover; refrigerate 10 minutes.
Heat oil in wok or large pan; stir-fry prawn mixture, in batches, until prawns are browned and cooked through.
Marinade Combine all ingredients in bowl; mix well.

Freeze Marinated prawns suitable

chicken stir-fry with
lemon sauce

1 tablespoon peanut oil

2 cloves garlic, crushed

5 (550g) chicken thigh fillets, chopped

500g packet frozen Chinese vegetables

Lemon Sauce

2 tablespoons lemon juice

1/2 chicken stock cube

1 tablespoon sugar

2 teaspoons dry sherry

1 teaspoon light soy sauce

1/4 teaspoon sweet chilli sauce

1 teaspoon cornflour

1/4 cup (60ml) water

Heat oil in wok or large pan; stir-fry garlic and chicken until chicken is browned lightly, remove from pan. Add vegetables to same pan; stir-fry for 5 minutes. Return chicken to pan with Lemon Sauce; stir-fry until heated through.

Lemon Sauce Combine juice, crumbled stock cube, sugar, sherry and sauces in pan, stir in blended cornflour and water. Stir over heat until sauce boils and thickens.

chicken with spicy
mango sauce

1 tablespoon peanut oil

5 (550g) chicken thigh fillets, sliced

300g broccoli, chopped

150g snow peas

1 tablespoon mild curry paste

1 tablespoon lime juice

½ chicken stock cube

½ cup (125ml) water

1 cup (250ml) coconut milk

1 tablespoon mango chutney

1 medium (430g) mango, sliced

⅓ cup (15g) flaked coconut, toasted

¼ cup chopped fresh coriander leaves

Heat oil in wok or large pan; stir-fry chicken, in batches, until browned.

Return chicken to pan with broccoli, snow peas, paste, juice, crumbled stock cube, water, coconut milk and chutney, stir over heat until mixture boils. Stir in mango; serve sprinkled with coconut and coriander.

24 fried noodles with
garlic pork

175g thin dried
egg noodles

2 tablespoons
vegetable oil

2 cloves garlic,
crushed

250g pork fillet,
chopped

1/2 cup (75g) chopped
unsalted roasted
peanuts

1/4 cup (30g)
dried shrimp

6 green onions,
chopped

2 tablespoons
fish sauce

1 teaspoon
brown sugar

1 small fresh red chilli,
chopped finely

2 tablespoons
lime juice

2 tablespoons
chopped fresh
coriander leaves

Add noodles to large pan of boiling water, boil,
uncovered, until just tender; drain.
Heat oil in wok or large pan; stir-fry garlic and
pork until browned. Add nuts, shrimp, onions,
sauce, sugar, chilli and juice to same pan;
stir-fry 1 minute.
Stir in noodles and coriander, stir-fry until
heated through.

Microwave Noodles suitable

cajun-style fish
salad

400g white fish fillets

1 teaspoon
dried thyme

1 teaspoon dried
parsley flakes

2 teaspoons garlic salt

1 teaspoon
hot paprika

1 teaspoon
onion powder

1/2 teaspoon cracked
black pepper

300g small yellow
squash, sliced

150g green beans,
sliced

1 tablespoon
vegetable oil

30g butter

few drops
Tabasco sauce

Cut fish into 3cm pieces; pat dry on absorbent paper. Add fish to
combined herbs and spices; mix well. Boil, steam or microwave squash
and beans, separately, until just tender; drain immediately. Rinse under
cold water; drain well.

Heat oil in wok or large pan; stir-fry fish, in batches, until tender. Return
fish to pan with squash, beans and butter; stir-fry until heated through.
Add Tabasco sauce to taste.

rice noodle
stir-fry

Place noodles in large heatproof bowl, cover with boiling water, stand 20 minutes or until tender; drain.
Heat half the oil in wok or large pan; stir-fry beef, in batches, until well browned. Heat remaining oil in same pan; stir-fry onions, garlic, capsicum and paste until capsicum is softened slightly.
Return beef to pan with noodles and remaining ingredients; stir-fry for 1 minute or until heated through.

150g thick rice stick noodles

2 tablespoons peanut oil

750g minced beef

6 green onions, chopped

2 cloves garlic, crushed

1 medium (200g) red capsicum, sliced thinly

1 medium (200g) yellow capsicum, sliced thinly

2 tablespoons green curry paste

2 tablespoons sweet chilli sauce

2 teaspoons fish sauce

1 cup (250ml) coconut milk

1/4 cup chopped fresh coriander leaves

lamb with basil

and vegetables

2 cloves garlic

2 large fresh
red chillies

1 medium (120g) carrot

1 medium (150g) onion

1 tablespoon
peanut oil

1 tablespoon
peanut oil, extra

1½ tablespoons
tandoori curry paste

500g lamb fillets,
sliced thinly

230g can sliced
bamboo shoots, drained

4 green onions,
chopped

⅓ cup shredded fresh
basil leaves

1 tablespoon
fish sauce

Cut garlic, chillies and carrot into thin strips. Cut onion in half and then into wedges.
Heat oil in wok or large pan; stir-fry garlic and chillies until lightly browned, remove from pan. Add onion to same pan; stir-fry until soft, remove from pan.
Heat extra oil in same pan, add curry paste, cook 1 minute; stir-fry lamb, in batches, until tender. Return lamb and onion to pan with carrot, bamboo shoots, green onions, basil and sauce; stir-fry until heated through. Serve lamb mixture topped with garlic and chilli.

28 stir-fried chicken
and noodles

200g thick rice stick noodles

1/4 cup (60ml) peanut oil

5 (550g) chicken thigh fillets, sliced thinly

250g asparagus, chopped

2 green onions, sliced

1 large (350g) yellow capsicum, sliced thinly

2 tablespoons crunchy peanut butter

2 tablespoons fish sauce

2 teaspoons sambal oelek

50g snow pea sprouts

Coriander Pesto

3/4 cup firmly packed fresh coriander leaves

2 cloves garlic, halved

1/2 cup (75g) unsalted roasted cashews

1/3 cup (30g) coconut milk powder

1 1/2 tablespoons lime juice

1 1/2 tablespoons peanut oil

Place noodles in large heatproof bowl, cover with boiling water, stand 20 minutes or until tender; drain.

Heat 2 tablespoons of the oil in wok or large pan; stir-fry chicken, in batches, until browned. Heat remaining oil in same pan; stir-fry asparagus, onions and capsicum until just tender. Return chicken to pan with Coriander Pesto, combined with peanut butter, sauce and sambal oelek, stir until combined. Add noodles and snow pea sprouts; stir-fry until heated through.

Coriander Pesto Process coriander, garlic and cashews until combined; add milk powder, process until just combined. Add juice and oil in a thin stream while motor is operating; process until mixture is creamy. Cover surface with plastic wrap.

30 chilli lime noodles

500g fresh
rice noodles

2 tablespoons
vegetable oil

2 medium (300g)
onions, sliced

2 cloves garlic,
crushed

350g minced pork

1 medium (200g) red
capsicum, sliced thinly

1/4 cup (60ml)
lime juice

2 tablespoons
soy sauce

1 tablespoon
fish sauce

1 tablespoon
oyster sauce

1 tablespoon sweet
chilli sauce

1 tablespoon grated
fresh ginger

2 green onions,
chopped

Place noodles in large bowl, cover with warm water, stand 5 minutes; drain.
Heat oil in wok or large pan; stir-fry onions and garlic until onions are soft. Add pork to pan; stir-fry until browned. Add capsicum, noodles, juice, sauces and ginger to same pan; stir-fry until heated through. Sprinkle with green onions.

saigon-style

noodles

375g thick rice
stick noodles

1 tablespoon
fish sauce

1/4 cup (60ml)
soy sauce

2 tablespoons
oyster sauce

1/4 cup (60ml)
lime juice

3 (330g) chicken thigh
fillets, sliced

250g pork fillet,
sliced thinly

700g medium
uncooked prawns,
shelled, halved

250g asparagus,
chopped

250g Chinese
broccoli, shredded

2 tablespoons
peanut oil

5 cloves garlic, crushed

4 green onions, sliced

1 cup (80g) bean
sprouts

2 tablespoons
chopped fresh
coriander leaves

Place noodles in bowl, cover with boiling water,
stand 20 minutes or until soft; drain. Combine
sauces with juice in jug. Combine chicken
and pork in bowl with half the sauce mixture.
Combine prawns with remaining sauce mixture
in separate bowl. Refrigerate bowls 10 minutes.
Drain mixtures; reserve marinades. Boil, steam
or microwave asparagus and broccoli, separately,
until tender; drain, rinse, drain.

Heat half the oil in wok or large pan; stir-fry
chicken and pork, in batches, until browned.
Heat remaining oil; stir-fry garlic, onions and
prawns until prawns are tender. Return chicken
and pork to pan with reserved marinades,
asparagus, broccoli and remaining ingredients;
stir-fry until mixture boils, boil 1 minute. Add
noodles, stir-fry until heated through.

baby corn
miniature corn
Small ears of corn about the size of a finger; should be a pale creamy yellow colour. Available fresh or canned. If using canned corn, drain liquid and add corn towards end of cooking. Fresh corn requires an extra few minutes' cooking.

snake beans
yard-long beans
Long, thin, fresh green beans. Colour and tender texture are similar to green beans. Stem ends should be removed before cooking.

bok choy
pak choi, baak choy, Chinese chard
Mild, slightly peppery taste. Both the thick white ribs and dark green leaves are edible, in stir-fries, soups and raw.

baby bok choy
Shanghai bok choy
Smaller and more tender than bok choy; sometimes used whole.

Chinese cabbage
Peking cabbage, wong bok, wong nga baak
Pale green, delicately flavoured cabbage, long in shape like cos lettuce. Can be eaten raw, stir-fried or braised.

Chinese broccoli
gai larn, Chinese kale
Long crunchy stems are chopped, then steamed, boiled, stir-fried or braised in oyster sauce. The dark green, coarse leaves are generally discarded.

Choy sum
flowering cabbage, flowering bok choy
One of the most common of the Chinese greens, choy sum's small yellow flowers, green stems and soft green leaves are all edible. Choy sum has a mild mustard-like flavor and can be steamed, stir-fried or braised with a little sesame oil.

coriander
cilantro,
Chinese parsley
A pungent herb available
everywhere these days;
all parts of the plant can
be used; the root is an
essential part of Thai
cooking. Dried ground
coriander or coriander seeds
cannot replace fresh coriander
leaves in recipes – the flavours are
completely different.

kaffir lime leaves
Aromatic leaves of a
small citrus tree
bearing a
bumpy
wrinkled-skinned
yellow-green fruit;
use fresh or dried
– dried are more readily
available. Leaves are fragrant
and provide a tangy taste to soups,
curries and stir-fries.

lemon grass
A tall, narrow grass with long,
sharp-edged leaves and a
lemony scent and flavour. Used
to flavour curries and soups
and is an important
component in curry
pastes. Only the pale,
lower part of the
stem should
be used.

oyster mushrooms
tree oyster mushroom,
abalone mushroom
A fan-shaped
mushroom with
a fluted cap
ranging from creamy
yellow to white-gray to
slightly salmon in colour.
Used predominantly in stir-fries,
its soft flesh and delicate flavour
is delicious.

shiitake mushrooms
fragrant mushrooms,
golden oak
mushrooms,
Chinese black
mushrooms
Grey in colour with
a rich spicy flavour.
Can be used dried or fresh.
Dried shiitake is commonly
used in Asian cooking, as the
flavour is more pronounced.
It reconstitutes well by soaking in
hot water for 20 minutes. Stem
should then be removed.

bean sprouts
Available from
greengrocers
and supermarkets,
bean sprouts are crunchy
and nutty in texture. `Tails' or
the thread-like roots can be
removed before cooking for
a neater appearance.

thai-style chicken curry

1 tablespoon
vegetable oil

1 tablespoon
red curry paste

5 (550g) chicken thigh
fillets, sliced

1 cup (250ml)
coconut milk

1 tablespoon
fish sauce

4 green onions, sliced

230g can sliced
bamboo shoots,
drained

1 tablespoon shredded
fresh basil

Heat oil in wok or
large pan; stir-fry
curry paste until
fragrant. Add chicken;
stir-fry, in batches,
until lightly browned.
Return chicken to
pan with coconut
milk, sauce, onions
and bamboo shoots;
simmer, uncovered,
about 5 minutes or
until chicken is tender.
Stir in basil.

36 prawns with hot spicy
pesto

Shell and devein prawns, leaving tails intact. Combine prawns and Hot Spicy Pesto in large bowl; mix well. Cut onions into thin wedges.

Heat oil in wok or large pan; stir-fry onions until just tender. Stir in prawn mixture and bean sprouts; stir-fry until prawns are just tender.

Hot Spicy Pesto Blend or process all ingredients until smooth.

1kg uncooked large prawns

2 medium (300g) onions

2 tablespoons vegetable oil

4 cups (320g) bean sprouts

hot spicy pesto

1/4 cup firmly packed fresh basil leaves

2 tablespoons fresh coriander leaves

1/4 cup (60ml) vegetable oil

2 teaspoons sambal oelek

4 cloves garlic, chopped

1 teaspoon chopped fresh ginger

2 tablespoons dry sherry

1 teaspoon sesame oil

honeyed beef and burghul

2 cups (320g) burghul

2 tablespoons olive oil

500g beef strips

2 teaspoons grated orange rind

3 cloves garlic, crushed

1 tablespoon honey

2 medium (340g) red onions, chopped

2 medium (400g) yellow capsicums, chopped

1 cup chopped fresh parsley

1/4 cup chopped fresh chives

1/4 cup chopped fresh mint leaves

2 tablespoons chopped fresh basil leaves

4 small (520g) tomatoes, chopped

1/4 cup (60ml) lemon juice

1 tablespoon red wine vinegar

Place burghul in heatproof bowl, cover with boiling water; stand 10 minutes. Drain burghul, rinse under cold water, drain; pat dry on absorbent paper.

Heat half the oil in wok or large pan; stir-fry combined beef, rind, garlic and honey, in batches, until beef is browned and cooked as desired.

Heat remaining oil in same pan; stir-fry onions and capsicum for 1 minute. Return beef to pan with burghul and remaining ingredients; stir-fry until hot.

mediterranean
octopus stir-fry

1kg baby octopus

2 tablespoons olive oil

2 medium (300g) onions, sliced

1 large (350g) yellow capsicum, chopped

2 large (500g) tomatoes, seeded, sliced

1/2 cup (60g) seeded black olives

1 tablespoon tomato paste

1/4 cup (60ml) dry red wine

1/4 cup (60ml) lemon juice

2 tablespoons brown sugar

2 cloves garlic, crushed

2 tablespoons chopped fresh oregano

2 bay leaves

2 teaspoons cornflour

1/4 cup (60ml) water

1/4 cup shredded fresh basil leaves

Remove and discard heads and beaks from octopus; cut octopus into quarters.

Heat half the oil in wok or large pan; stir-fry octopus, in batches, until just tender.

Heat remaining oil in same pan; stir-fry onions and capsicum until onions are just soft. Add tomatoes; stir-fry 1 minute. Return octopus to pan with olives, paste, wine, juice, sugar, garlic, oregano, bay leaves and blended cornflour and water; stir over heat until mixture boils and thickens slightly.

Discard bay leaves; stir in basil.

40 stir-fried seafood

with basil

200g white fish fillets

8 green-lipped mussels

250g uncooked large prawns

100g squid hoods

2 cloves garlic, crushed

1 large fresh red chilli, chopped

1 tablespoon chopped fresh coriander root

1/4 cup (60ml) vegetable oil

100g scallops

2 tablespoons oyster sauce

2 tablespoons fish sauce

1 medium (200g) red capsicum, sliced

8 green onions, chopped

1/3 cup shredded fresh basil leaves

Cut fish into 2cm pieces. Scrub mussels; remove beards. Shell prawns, leaving tails intact. Cut squid hoods open, score shallow diagonal slashes in criss-cross pattern on inside surface; cut into 4cm squares.

Grind garlic, chilli and coriander root to a paste using a mortar and pestle.

Heat oil in wok or large pan, add coriander paste; cook, stirring, until fragrant.

Add seafood to same pan; stir-fry until all seafood is just tender. Add sauces, capsicum, onions and basil; stir-fry 2 minutes.

mongolian

garlic lamb

1kg lamb fillets, sliced thinly

1 teaspoon five-spice powder

2 teaspoons sugar

1 tablespoon cornflour

1/3 cup (80ml) light soy sauce

1 tablespoon black bean sauce

3 cloves garlic, crushed

1 1/2 tablespoons rice vinegar

1 egg, beaten lightly

1/4 cup (60ml) peanut oil

3 medium (450g) onions, sliced

1/3 cup (80ml) beef stock

1/4 teaspoon sesame oil

2 green onions, sliced thinly

Place lamb in large bowl with combined spice, sugar, cornflour, half the sauces, the garlic, vinegar and egg. Cover; refrigerate 10 minutes.

Drain lamb over small bowl; reserve marinade. Heat half the peanut oil in wok or large pan; stir-fry lamb, in batches, until browned and tender.

Heat remaining peanut oil in same pan; stir-fry onions until soft.

Return lamb to pan with reserved marinade, remaining sauces, stock and sesame oil; stir over heat until mixture boils and thickens. Serve sprinkled with onions.

42 chilli beef
and spinach

1 tablespoon peanut oil

400g beef strips

2 small fresh red chillies, chopped

1 clove garlic, crushed

500g spinach, chopped

2 teaspoons teriyaki sauce

1 teaspoon sugar

1 teaspoon cornflour

$^1/_2$ beef stock cube

$^1/_4$ cup (60ml) water

Heat oil in wok or large pan; stir-fry combined beef, chillies and garlic, in batches, until beef is browned. Return beef to pan with spinach, sauce and sugar; stir-fry 1 minute.

Add blended remaining ingredients; stir over heat until mixture boils and thickens.

caramelised chicken
wings

12 large (1.5kg) chicken wings

2 tablespoons peanut oil

3 cloves garlic, crushed

1 tablespoon chopped
fresh ginger

1 tablespoon fish sauce

1 tablespoon soy sauce

1/4 cup (60ml) honey

2 green onions, chopped

Remove and discard tip from each wing. Cut wings in half at joint.
Heat oil in wok or large pan; stir-fry garlic, ginger and chicken for 5 minutes. Add sauces and honey; mix well. Cook, covered, about 10 minutes or until chicken is lightly browned and tender, stirring occasionally. Serve sprinkled with green onions.

44 braised chicken on crisp noodles

12 (20g) Chinese
dried mushrooms

2 tablespoons
peanut oil

6 (660g) chicken thigh
fillets, sliced thinly

1 bunch (400g) spring
onions, quartered

3 cloves garlic,
crushed

2 teaspoons grated
fresh ginger

1 medium (200g) red
capsicum, sliced

2 (300g) baby bok
choy, chopped

1 teaspoon sugar

1 tablespoon
oyster sauce

2 tablespoons
light soy sauce

2 teaspoons cornflour

1/4 cup (60ml) water

500g Hokkien noodles

vegetable oil,
for deep-frying

2 tablespoons
chopped fresh chives

Place mushrooms in medium heatproof bowl, cover with boiling water; stand 20 minutes. Drain mushrooms, discard stems, slice caps.

Heat half the peanut oil in wok or large pan; stir-fry chicken, in batches, until browned and tender.

Heat remaining peanut oil in same pan; stir-fry onions, garlic, ginger and capsicum until onions are soft and browned lightly. Return chicken to pan with mushrooms, bok choy, sugar and sauces; stir in blended cornflour and water. Stir over heat until mixture boils and thickens.

Deep-fry noodles in hot vegetable oil, in batches, until golden and crisp; drain on absorbent paper. Serve chicken and vegetable mixture on noodles, sprinkled with chives.

barbecued **pork**

and noodles

375g thin fresh
egg noodles

1/4 cup (60ml)
vegetable oil

2 cloves garlic,
crushed

150g Chinese
barbecued pork, sliced

150g cooked
shelled prawns

2 sticks celery,
chopped

2 green onions,
chopped

2 tablespoons chopped
fresh coriander leaves

1/4 cup (60ml) sweet
chilli sauce

2 tablespoons black
bean sauce

1 tablespoon salt-
reduced soy sauce

Cut noodles into
15cm lengths. Rinse
noodles under cold
water; drain.

Heat oil in wok or large
pan; stir-fry garlic,
pork, prawns and
celery for 2 minutes.
Add noodles; stir-fry
until combined. Add
onions, coriander and
sauces; stir-fry until
heated through.

lemon grass

beef with asparagus

500g beef fillet, sliced thinly

3 cloves garlic, crushed

2 tablespoons finely chopped fresh lemon grass

1 teaspoon sugar

1 teaspoon salt

2 tablespoons peanut oil

250g asparagus, halved

1 large (200g) onion, cut into wedges

1 teaspoon grated fresh ginger

2 medium (380g) tomatoes, cut into wedges

2 tablespoons unsalted roasted peanuts, chopped

2 teaspoons fresh coriander leaves

Combine beef, garlic, lemon grass, sugar, salt and half the oil in large bowl, mix well. Cover; refrigerate 10 minutes.

Boil, steam or microwave asparagus until just tender, rinse under cold water, drain. Heat remaining oil in wok or large pan; stir-fry onion and ginger until onion is soft, remove from pan. Add beef to same pan, in batches; stir-fry until browned. Return beef to pan with onion mixture, tomatoes, asparagus and peanuts; stir-fry until heated through. Serve sprinkled with coriander.

Freeze Marinated beef suitable
Microwave Asparagus suitable

48 satay beef stir-fry

2 tablespoons soy sauce

1/2 cup (130g) crunchy peanut butter

1 teaspoon grated lemon rind

1 tablespoon lemon juice

1/2 teaspoon dried crushed chillies

1 clove garlic, crushed

2 teaspoons brown sugar

3/4 cup (180ml) coconut milk

1 medium (150g) onion, chopped

1 teaspoon ground cumin

1 teaspoon ground turmeric

2 tablespoons chopped fresh coriander leaves

1 tablespoons peanut oil

500g beef strips

2 tablespoons chopped unsalted roasted peanuts

230g can water chestnuts, drained, sliced

125g oyster mushrooms, sliced

4 green onions, sliced

Combine half the sauce with peanut butter, rind, juice, chilli, garlic, sugar and half the coconut milk in small pan; stir over low heat, without boiling, until heated through.

Process onion, remaining sauce, spices and coriander until smooth.

Heat oil in wok or large pan; stir-fry combined beef and onion paste, in batches, until beef is browned. Return beef to pan with remaining coconut milk and remaining ingredients; stir over heat until hot. Serve stir-fry with warm peanut sauce.

50 pork and noodles with
plum sauce

Combine sauces with ginger and garlic in jar. Combine half the sauce mixture with pork in large bowl. Rinse noodles under hot water; drain.

Heat oil in wok or large pan; stir-fry undrained pork, in batches, until browned and tender.

Add vegetables and noodles to same pan; stir-fry until vegetables are just tender. Return pork to pan with remaining plum sauce mixture and stock; stir-fry until mixture comes to the boil.

½ cup (125ml) plum sauce

2 tablespoons salt-reduced soy sauce

¼ cup (60ml) sweet chilli sauce

1 tablespoon grated fresh ginger

2 cloves garlic, crushed

500g pork fillets, sliced

500g Hokkien noodles

1 tablespoon peanut oil

200g sugar snap peas

1 medium (120g) carrot, sliced

1 medium (200g) red capsicum, sliced

200g button mushrooms, sliced

½ cup (125ml) chicken stock

*100g rice vermicelli
noodles*

6 green onions

*1 small (150g)
red capsicum*

2 sticks celery

*1 medium (120g)
zucchini*

*2 tablespoons
peanut oil*

*750g veal leg
steaks, sliced*

*150g button
mushrooms*

200g snow peas

*425g can baby
corn, drained*

*1¼ cups (100g)
bean sprouts*

1 tablespoon cornflour

¼ cup (60ml) water

*2 tablespoons light
soy sauce*

*1 tablespoon
oyster sauce*

*2 tablespoons
dry sherry*

Place noodles in large heatproof bowl, cover with boiling water, stand 5 minutes; drain.

Cut onions, capsicum, celery and zucchini into long thin strips.

Heat oil in wok or large pan; stir-fry veal, in batches, until browned.

Add onions, capsicum and celery to same pan; stir-fry 2 minutes.

Add zucchini, mushrooms, snow peas, corn and bean sprouts to pan; stir-fry 1 minute. Return veal to pan with noodles.

Add blended cornflour, water, sauces and sherry to pan; stir over heat until mixture boils and thickens.

52 chilli beef with
vermicelli

Place noodles in large heatproof bowl, cover with boiling water, stand 5 minutes; drain, keep warm.
Heat oil in wok or large pan; stir-fry onion, garlic and ginger until onion is soft. Add curry powder, spices and chillies to same pan; stir-fry until fragrant.
Add beef; stir-fry until well browned. Stir in water, crumbled stock cube and coconut milk powder; simmer, uncovered, about 8 minutes or until most of the liquid has evaporated.
Add coriander and tomatoes; stir-fry until heated through. Serve with warm noodles.

250g rice vermicelli noodles

1 tablespoon vegetable oil

1 medium (150g) onion, sliced

2 cloves garlic, crushed

1 teaspoon grated fresh ginger

1½ tablespoons mild curry powder

¼ teaspoon hot paprika

2 teaspoons ground cumin

¼ teaspoon chilli powder

2 small fresh red chillies, chopped finely

800g minced beef

1¾ cups (430ml) water

1 small chicken stock cube

2 tablespoons instant coconut milk powder

¼ cup chopped fresh coriander leaves

2 small (260g) tomatoes, chopped

Freeze Suitable
Microwave Suitable

with vegetable chunks

Boil, steam or microwave pumpkin and potatoes, separately, until just tender; drain. Quarter capsicum, remove seeds and membranes. Roast under grill or in very hot oven, skin-side up, until skin blisters and blackens. Cover capsicum pieces with plastic or paper for 5 minutes, peel away skin. Process capsicum, butter, nuts, garlic, parsley, pepper and juice until combined.

Heat oil in wok or large pan; stir-fry lamb, in batches, until browned. Return lamb to pan with pumpkin, potatoes, capsicum mixture and spinach; stir-fry until spinach is just wilted.

500g butternut pumpkin, cubed

4 small (480g) potatoes, sliced thickly

1 medium (200g) red capsicum

60g soft butter

2 tablespoons pine nuts, toasted

1 clove garlic, crushed

1/2 cup fresh parsley sprigs

1 teaspoon cracked black pepper

1 tablespoon lemon juice

2 teaspoons olive oil

400g lamb fillets, sliced thinly

500g spinach, chopped roughly

54 gingered fish stir-fry

750g white fish fillets, chopped

¾ cup (110g) cornflour

vegetable oil, for shallow-frying

2 medium (240g) carrots

1 tablespoon peanut oil

1 medium (150g) onion, chopped

1 medium (200g) red capsicum, chopped

1 medium (200g) green capsicum, chopped

4 cups (320g) bean sprouts

4 green onions, chopped

2 teaspoons cornflour, extra

2 teaspoons water

Marinade

1 tablespoon grated fresh ginger

2 cloves garlic, crushed

⅓ cup (80ml) light soy sauce

2 tablespoons white vinegar

2 tablespoons sweet sherry

2 tablespoons water

2 teaspoons brown sugar

Combine fish and Marinade in bowl, mix well. Cover; refrigerate 10 minutes. Drain fish from Marinade; reserve Marinade.

Toss fish in cornflour, then shallow-fry, in hot vegetable oil, until crisp and tender; remove and drain on absorbent paper.

Cut carrots into thin strips. Heat peanut oil in wok or large pan; stir-fry onion until soft. Add carrots, capsicum, sprouts and green onions to pan; stir-fry for 2 minutes. Stir in blended extra cornflour and water with reserved Marinade; stir over heat until mixture boils and thickens. Add fish to same pan; stir-fry gently until heated through.

Marinade Press ginger between 2 spoons, over small bowl, to extract juice; discard pulp. Stir in remaining ingredients; mix well.

56 red curry vegetable
noodles

500g Hokkien noodles

1 large (300g) red onion

1/4 cup (60ml) peanut oil

2 cloves garlic, crushed

2 teaspoons red curry paste

250g small yellow squash, quartered

1 medium (200g) yellow capsicum, chopped

1 medium (200g) red capsicum, chopped

125g sugar snap peas

1 cup (250ml) coconut milk

1 tablespoon lime juice

1/2 cup chopped fresh coriander leaves

Rinse noodles under hot water; drain. Cut onion into thin wedges. Heat oil in wok or large pan; stir-fry onion, garlic, paste and squash until onion is soft.

Add noodles, capsicum and peas to same pan; stir-fry until vegetables are almost tender. Stir in combined coconut milk, juice and coriander; cook, stirring, until mixture boils.

thai-style beef

and spinach stir-fry

2 tablespoons
peanut oil

2 medium (300g)
onions, sliced

3 cloves garlic,
crushed

1 tablespoon grated
fresh ginger

1 large (350g) red
capsicum, sliced

500g beef strips

500g spinach

$1/2$ cup firmly packed
fresh mint leaves

$1/3$ cup (50g) chopped
unsalted roasted
peanuts, toasted

1 tablespoon chopped
fresh lemon grass

2 fresh kaffir lime
leaves, shredded

2 teaspoons sugar

1 tablespoon
fish sauce

$1/4$ cup (60ml)
lime juice

$1/2$ teaspoon
sesame oil

Heat half the peanut oil in wok or large pan;
stir-fry onions, garlic and ginger until onions
are just soft. Add capsicum; stir-fry until just
soft, remove from pan.

Heat remaining peanut oil in same pan; stir-fry
beef, in batches, until browned and almost
cooked. Return beef to pan with spinach, mint,
peanuts, vegetable mixture and remaining
ingredients; stir-fry until spinach is just wilted
and mixture is heated through.

chow mein

350g thin fresh egg noodles

vegetable oil, for deep-frying

1 tablespoon peanut oil

2 (340g) chicken breast
fillets, sliced

500g uncooked medium
prawns, shelled

2 cloves garlic, crushed

2 teaspoons grated
fresh ginger

1 medium (150g)
onion, sliced

125g Chinese barbecued
pork, sliced thinly

1 medium (200g) red
capsicum, sliced thinly

125g snow peas, sliced thinly

4 Chinese cabbage
leaves, shredded

1/4 cup (50g) canned drained
bamboo shoots, sliced

4 green onions, sliced

1 1/2 cups (120g) bean sprouts

2 tablespoons salt-reduced
soy sauce

3 teaspoons hoisin sauce

2 teaspoons cornflour

1/2 cup (125ml) chicken stock

Deep-fry noodles in hot vegetable oil until puffed and browned lightly; drain on absorbent paper.

Heat half the peanut oil in wok or large pan; stir-fry chicken, in batches, until browned and tender. Chop chicken coarsely. Add prawns to same pan; stir-fry until just tender, remove.

Heat remaining peanut oil in same pan; stir-fry garlic, ginger and onion until onion is just soft. Return chicken and prawns to pan with pork, capsicum, snow peas, cabbage, bamboo shoots, green onions and sprouts; stir-fry until combined.

Stir in sauces and blended cornflour and stock; stir over heat until mixture boils and thickens. Serve over fried noodles.

glossary

bean sprouts also known as bean shoots.

beef

minced: also known as ground beef.

strips: prepared from blade, tenderloin, rib-eye, round, rump, sirloin and topside.

black beans fermented, salted and dried soy beans. Soak, drain and rinse dried beans; chop before cooking or mash during cooking to release flavour.

black bean sauce made from fermented soy beans, spices, water and flour.

burghul wheat that is steamed until partly cooked, cracked, then dried.

capsicum also known as bell pepper.

chillies available in many different types and sizes. Use rubber gloves when seeding and chopping fresh chillies as they can burn your skin. Removing seeds and membranes lessens the heat level.

powder: the Asian variety is the hottest, made from ground chillies; it can be used as a substitute for fresh chillies in the proportion of ½ teaspoon ground chilli powder to 1 medium chopped fresh chilli.

sweet chilli sauce: a mild commercial sauce made from red chillies, sugar, garlic and vinegar.

chinese barbecued pork also known as char siew. Traditionally cooked in special ovens, this pork has a sweet-sticky coating made from soy sauce, sherry, five-spice and hoisin sauce. It is available from Asian food stores.

chinese barbecue sauce a thick, sweet and salty commercial sauce used in marinades; made from fermented soy beans, vinegar, garlic, pepper and various spices. Available from Asian food stores.

chinese sausages highly spiced, bright red, thin pork sausages. The meat is preserved by the high spice content and can be kept at room temperature.

coconut

flaked: dried flaked coconut flesh.

instant milk powder: coconut milk that has been dehydrated and ground to a fine powder.

milk: pure, unsweetened coconut milk available in cans.

fish sauce also called nam pla or nuoc nam; made from pulverised, salted, fermented fish, most often anchovies. Has a pungent smell and strong taste.

five-spice powder mixture of ground cinnamon, cloves, star anise, Sichuan pepper and fennel seeds.

ginger, fresh also known as green or root ginger.

hoisin sauce a thick, sweet and spicy Chinese paste made from salted fermented soy beans, onions and garlic.

lamb

eye of loin: a cut derived from a row of loin chops. Once the bone and fat are removed, the larger portion is referred to as the eye of the loin.

fillet: tenderloin; the smaller piece of meat from a row of loin chops or cutlets.

noodles

bean thread vermicelli: also called cellophane noodles, made from green mung bean flour.

dried egg: fettuccine and tagliatelle are common dried egg noodles.

fresh egg: made from wheat flour and eggs; strands vary in thickness.

fresh rice: thick, wide, almost white in colour; made from rice and vegetable oil. Must be covered with boiling water to remove starch and excess oil before using in soups and stir-fries.

hokkien: a fresh wheat flour noodle; looks like a thicker, yellow-brown spaghetti. Sometimes referred to as stir-fry noodles.

rice vermicelli: also known as rice-flour noodles and rice stick noodles, made from rice flour and either deep-fried or soaked and used in stir-fries and soups.

thick rice stick: only differ from dried rice noodle in that they are thicker.

udon: Japanese broad white wheat noodles; available fresh or dried.

oil

olive: a mono-unsaturated oil, made from the pressing of tree-ripened olives. Extra Light or Light describes the mild flavour, not the fat levels.

peanut: pressed from ground peanuts; most commonly used oil in Asian cooking because of its high smoke point.

sesame: made from roasted, crushed, white sesame seeds; a flavouring rather than a cooking medium.

vegetable: any of a number of oils sourced from plants rather than animal fats.

onion

green: also known as scallion or (incorrectly) shallot; an immature onion picked before the bulb has formed, having a long, bright-green edible stalk.

spring: has a crisp, narrow green-leafed top and a fairly large, sweet-tasting, white bulb.

oyster sauce rich, brown sauce made from oysters, brine, salt and soy sauce then thickened with starch.

plum sauce a thick, sweet and sour dipping sauce made from plums, vinegar, sugar, chillies and spices.

pork

butterfly: skinless, boneless mid-loin chop, split in half and flattened.

fillet: skinless, boneless eye-fillet cut from the loin.

minced: ground pork.

strips: lean pork leg steak or schnitzel cut into strips.

prawns also known as shrimp.

sambal oelek (also ulek) Indonesian in origin; a salty paste made from ground chillies, sugar and spices.

seafood sticks made from processed Alaskan pollack flavoured with crab.

sichuan pepper also known as Chinese pepper. Small, red-brown aromatic seeds, resembling black peppercorns; they have a peppery-lemon flavour.

snow peas also called mange tout ("eat all").

stock 1 cup (250ml) stock is equivalent to 1 cup (250ml) water plus 1 crumbled stock cube (or 1 teaspoon stock powder).

sugar snap peas

small pods with small, formed peas inside; they are eaten whole, cooked or raw.

teriyaki

sauce a commercially bottled sauce usually made from soy sauce,

mirin, sugar, ginger and other spices.

tofu also known as bean curd, an off-white custard-like product made from the "milk" of crushed soy beans; comes fresh as firm or silken, and processed as fried or pressed dried sheets. Leftover fresh tofu can be refrigerated in water (which is changed daily) for up to 4 days.

vinegar

red: ingredients include water, rice, glutinous rice and food colouring.

rice: made from fermented rice; colourless and flavoured with sugar and salt.

yogurt, plain whole cow milk yogurt has been used in these recipes unless stated otherwise.

zucchini also known as courgette.

These conversions are approximate only, but the difference between an exact and the approximate conversion of various liquid and dry measures is minimal and will not affect your cooking results.

Note: NZ, Canada, US and UK all use 15ml tablespoons. Australian tablespoons measure 20ml. All cup and spoon measurements are level.

Measuring equipment

The difference between one country's measuring cups and another's is, at most, within a 2 or 3 teaspoon variance. (For the record, 1 Australian metric measuring cup holds approximately 250ml.) The most accurate way of measuring dry ingredients is to weigh them. For liquids, use a clear glass or plastic jug having metric markings.

How to measure

When using graduated measuring cups, shake dry ingredients loosely into the appropriate cup. Do not tap the cup on a bench or tightly pack the ingredients unless directed to do so. Level the top of measuring cups and measuring spoons with a knife. When measuring liquids, place a clear glass or plastic jug having metric markings on a flat surface to check accuracy at eye level.

Dry measures

metric	imperial
15g	½oz
30g	1oz
60g	2oz
90g	3oz
125g	4oz (¼lb)
155g	5oz
185g	6oz
220g	7oz
250g	8oz (½lb)
280g	9oz
315g	10oz
345g	11oz
375g	12oz (¾lb)
410g	13oz
440g	14oz
470g	15oz
500g	16oz (1lb)
750g	24oz (1½lb)
1kg	32oz (2lb)

We use large eggs with an average weight of 60g.

Liquid measures

metric	imperial
30 ml	1 fluid oz
60 ml	2 fluid oz
100 ml	3 fluid oz
125 ml	4 fluid oz
150 ml	5 fluid oz (¼ pint/1 gill)
190 ml	6 fluid oz
250 ml (1cup)	8 fluid oz
300 ml	10 fluid oz (½ pint)
500 ml	16 fluid oz
600 ml	20 fluid oz (1 pint)
1000 ml (1litre)	1¾ pints

Helpful measures

metric	imperial
3mm	⅛in
6mm	¼in
1cm	½in
2cm	¾in
2.5cm	1in
6cm	2½in
8cm	3in
20cm	8in
23cm	9in
25cm	10in
30cm	12in (1ft)

Oven temperatures

These oven temperatures are only a guide for conventional ovens. For fan-forced ovens, check the manufacturer's manual.

	°C (Celsius)	°F (Fahrenheit)	Gas Mark
Very slow	120	250	½
Slow	150	275 – 300	1 – 2
Moderately slow	160	325	3
Moderate	180	350 – 375	4 – 5
Moderately hot	200	400	6
Hot	220	425 – 450	7 – 8
Very hot	240	475	9

ARE YOU MISSING SOME OF THE WORLD'S FAVOURITE COOKBOOKS?

The Australian Women's Weekly cookbooks are available from bookshops, cookshops, supermarkets and other stores all over the world. You can also buy direct from the publisher, using the order form below.

Mini Series £2.50 190x138mm 64 pages			
	QTY		QTY
4 Fast Ingredients		Italian	
15-minute Feasts		Jams & Jellies	
30-minute Meals		Kids Party Food	
50 Fast Chicken Fillets		Last-minute Meals	
After-work Stir-fries		Lebanese Cooking	
Barbecue		Malaysian Favourites	
Barbecue Chicken		Microwave	
Barbecued Seafood		Mince	
Biscuits, Brownies & Biscotti		Muffins	
Bites		Noodles	
Bowl Food		Party Food	
Burgers, Rösti & Fritters		Pasta	
Cafe Cakes		Pickles and Chutneys	
Cafe Food		Potatoes	
Casseroles		Risotto	
Char-grills & Barbecues		Roast	
Cheesecakes, Pavlovas & Trifles		Salads	
Chocolate		Seafood	
Chocolate Cakes		Simple Slices	
Christmas Cakes & Puddings		Simply Seafood	
Cocktails		Skinny Food	
Curries		Stir-fries	
Drinks		Summer Salads	
Fast Fish		Tapas, Antipasto & Mezze	
Fast Food for Friends		Thai Cooking	
Fast Soup		Thai Favourites	
Finger Food		Vegetarian	
From the Shelf		Vegetarian Stir-fries	
Gluten-free Cooking		Vegie Main Meals	
Ice-creams & Sorbets		Wok	
Indian Cooking		**TOTAL COST**	**£**

NAME

ADDRESS

POSTCODE

DAYTIME PHONE

I ENCLOSE MY CHEQUE/MONEY ORDER FOR £

OR PLEASE CHARGE MY VISA, ACCESS OR MASTERCARD NUMBER

CARDHOLDER'S NAME

EXPIRY DATE

CARDHOLDER'S SIGNATURE

To order: Mail or fax – photocopy or complete the order form above, and send your credit card details or cheque payable to: Australian Consolidated Press (UK), Moulton Park Business Centre, Red House Road, Moulton Park, Northampton NN3 6AQ, phone (+44) (01) 604 497531, fax (+44) (01) 604 497533, e-mail books@acpuk.com. Or order online at **www.acpuk.com**
Non-UK residents: We accept the credit cards listed on the coupon, or cheques, drafts or International Money Orders payable in sterling and drawn on a UK bank. Credit card charges are at the exchange rate current at the time of payment.
Postage and packing UK: Add £1.00 per order plus 25p per book.
Postage and packing overseas: Add £2.00 per order plus 50p per book.
Offer ends 31.12.2006

Food director Pamela Clark
Associate food editor Karen Hammial
Asisstant food editor Kathy McGarry
Assistant recipe editor Elizabeth Hooper
ACP BOOKS
Editorial director Susan Tomnay
Creative director Hieu Chi Nguyen
Senior editor Julie Collard
Concept design Jackie Richards
Designer Jackie Richards
Sales director Brian Cearnes
Brand manager Renée Crea
Production manager Carol Currie
Chief executive officer John Alexander
Group publisher Pat Ingram
Publisher Sue Wannan
Editorial director (AWW) Deborah Thomas

Produced by ACP Books, Sydney.
Printing by Dai Nippon Printing in Korea.
Published by ACP Publishing Pty Limited,
54 Park St, Sydney;
GPO Box 4088, Sydney, NSW 2001.
Ph: (02) 9282 8618 Fax: (02) 9267 9438.
acpbooks@acp.com.au
www.acpbooks.com.au
To order books phone 136 116.
Send recipe enquiries to
Recipeenquiries@acp.com.au
RIGHTS ENQUIRIES
Laura Bamford, Director ACP Books.
lbamford@acplon.co.uk
Ph: +44 (207) 812 6526
Australia Distributed by Network Services,
GPO Box 4088, Sydney, NSW 1028.
Ph: (02) 9282 8777 Fax: (02) 9264 3278.
United Kingdom Distributed by Australian
Consolidated Press (UK), Moulton Park Busine
Centre, Red House Road, Moulton Park,
Northampton, NN3 6AQ. Ph: (01604) 497 53
Fax: (01604) 497 533 acpukltd@aol.com
Canada Distributed by Whitecap Books Ltd,
351 Lynn Ave, North Vancouver, BC, V7J 2C4
Ph: (604) 980 9852 Fax: (604) 980 8197
customerservice@whitecap.ca
www.whitecap.ca
New Zealand Distributed by Netlink Distributic
Company, ACP Media Centre, Cnr Fanshawe
and Beaumont Streets, Westhaven, Auckland.
PO Box 47906, Ponsonby, Auckland, NZ.
Ph: (9) 366 9966 ask@ndcnz.co.nz
South Africa Distributed by PSD Promotions,
30 Diesel Road, Isando, Gauteng, Johannesb
PO Box 1175, Isando, 1600, Gauteng, Johanne
Ph: (27 11) 392 6065/7 Fax: (27 11) 392 6079
orders@psdprom.co.za

Clark, Pamela.
The Australian Women's Weekly
Stir-fries

Includes index.
ISBN 1 86396 096 1

1. Stir-frying. I. Title: Australian Women's Weekl
641.77

© ACP Publishing Pty Limited 1998
ABN 18 053 273 546

First published 1998.
Reprinted 1999, 2000, 2001, 2005.

Cover Lemon grass beef with asparagus, pa
Stylist Vicki Liley
Photographer Scott Cameron
Back cover at left, Red curry vegetable nood
page 56; at right, Mustard pork with olives and
artichokes, page 13.